Fresh Paint

A Memoir of Adoption

Lori Adams

Photos by the author

PRESS

Fresh Paint

A Memoir of Adoption

Table of Contents

Dedication

This book is dedicated to my parents, Frank and Joy Adams, who were the first people to teach me about loving unconditionally. Thank you, Mom and Dad, for that special gift.

To Kevin and Craig, this is your story. I love you forever.

Introduction

◠͜

I used to think that in order to come full circle as a woman, I needed to have my own baby. Being a mother is something I had always wanted to be. When I first laid eyes on Daniel, after my emergency c-section, I thought that it was my defining moment: I had given birth. As I came out of the anesthetic, I looked down at my baby lying on my chest. As he cried and fussed, I began to sing to him, and he immediately stopped to look into my eyes. Even though there were others in the room, it seemed like it was just the two of us there, together for the first time after so many months of waiting. With his little body against mine, his skin on my skin, I watched him gently rise with the rhythm of my breathing. I felt his human presence as he responded to my voice. My soul opened to him. It was one of the most precious moments of my adult life . . . one that I will always cherish.

Two years later, Mitchell was born after another high-risk pregnancy and long labor. Jeff and I were thrilled that he came into this world looking like a carbon copy of his father. We had made two beautiful sons. Although we were totally smitten with Mitchell, I had secretly wondered, how could I possibly love Mitch as much as I loved Daniel? I soon found out that I had enough within me to share with both of them. It is possible to love the new one as much as the first. That intimate connection did happen again. My soul opened twice.

Little did I know that just over a year later, my mind would be contemplating this situation once again as I prepared to add another to our family through adoption. The following are my personal memories of the incredible journey. Italicized sections chronicle my deepest thoughts and emotions as I went through the process of becoming a mother in this special way.

Please note that the events that occurred are true, but some names have been changed. This account is my own personal observation. The intimate details of the process I experienced are not meant to be a representation of all adoptions. Every adoption experience is as unique as every adopted child.

I'm hopeful that my story will stir something within you.

Lori

Early Thoughts

April 1997

Dear me,

Dan and Mitch are growing fast out of the toddler stage into little boys. I am feeling extremely lucky being their mommy. I love that my days are so full with them, being there to just watch them learn and grow. They feel safe and content whenever I am near. I am who they run to when they have a need or want to be comforted. It gives me a great sense of inner strength to know that I am the one they usually choose. I am their mother. Now, I know what that means.

Lately, we have been talking about adopting another child. Jeff and I have been looking at this as an option since we found out about our fertility problems. Now that God has given us two miracles, what would it be like to increase our family even more? I definitely want another baby someday, but I don't necessarily want to be pregnant again. I've already been there twice, and I really don't feel the need to do it again. It took a lot out of me physically, and I am considered high risk from now on.

This house is already in the little-tyke mode. Now would be a great time to add to our family since the boys are so young. Adopting a baby would be great if it happened right now. But, here's the kicker. We'll be in for a *very long* wait for an infant. I had no idea that there are so many other couples looking to adopt. It's unbelievable. Catholic Social

Services told me that we would probably have to wait at least six years for an infant because we already have biological children. That seems crazy to me. We went to the foster parenting workshop where we learned that if we become foster parents, there's a chance that we'll have to give the child back to his/her birthparents. That would kill me to have to let go. Furthermore, I don't think I want to be in constant contact with a birth family. What if there is so much dysfunction that it causes problems? Truthfully, I just don't think I want to share. We want to be a forever family.

Foreign adoption seems to be the way to go. We found a lot of information about it on the web. Our friend Jodi recommended a good agency in Grand Rapids. Their little girl, Asia, is just beautiful. Here we go . . .

August 1997

Hi me,

The paperwork process has begun. Sarah, our social worker, told us it would be a minimum of six to nine months to get a referral for the Russia program. Daniel and Mitchell are only four and two; good ages to introduce a new baby. Mom and Dad are very supportive, as are Jeff's parents. My sisters think it's a beautiful idea. They all know there is much to share around here.

I'm wondering about what the baby is going to look like and who he or she will be. So far, I've received what appears to me as two signs from above that this is meant to be.

First sign:

Last month, Jeff and I sat at the kitchen table late one night to fill out the adoption contract and preliminary paperwork. We had a good heart-to-heart discussion about what it's going to be like to go to Russia and adopt. How healthy will the baby be? What are the conditions of the orphanages over there? What kind of life or genetics will this child have come from? We wondered out loud. Do Russian people even like Americans in general? Just then the show *Nightline* came on the television. We were startled by the subject of the show: "Life in a Russian orphanage." Of course, we taped it, and watched it again and again.

Second sign:

A couple of weeks ago at the salon, I shared with my stylist that we had started the paperwork and were waiting to adopt from Russia. She told me about one of her other clients whose daughter had just adopted a little girl from there. The phone rang, and it was that very woman, calling to set up an appointment. When she told her about our conversation, the woman drove over to the salon and spent the next hour educating me about her daughter's experience. Normally, people just don't do this. This is going to be a special journey. I can feel it.

Still, I am a little anxious about what the reality will be like. Will this child be an easy baby? Will it matter to me if the baby doesn't look anything like us? Will I be able to connect with him or her as deeply as I love Dan and Mitch? Probably, but this will be different. After carrying the boys inside me and being there since they took their first breath, I know those two better than anyone. Being their mother is the deepest connection that I've ever experienced. It's primal. While in the hospital after Daniel's birth, I heard a cry from the nursery and although I couldn't see him, I instinctively knew his little voice. I have always been able to recognize him and Mitchell just by the way they smell. It's an amazing phenomenon, and one of the many intuitive gifts God gives us when He makes us mothers. I really want to achieve that same connection with the new baby. I just don't know if it will happen. The baby will be someone else's child, and representing another gene pool altogether. Will I really think of him or her as mine? Really and truly? And what if the child doesn't bond with me in those first months or years? I need to remember what Grandma Adams told me. "You're only pregnant for nine months, and then the real work of your life begins." She was so right. I'll still be my baby's mother; it's just that we won't be together for the first months. I need to think of this time as a kind of pregnancy . . . that's the stage I'm in right now. I'm really open to all of it. I want to share more of myself, but still, I'm a little scared.

December 1997

Hi,
It's so fun around here with little ones. There's magic in the air. I'm listening to the Christmas song I recorded with Daniel and Mitch last year, *All About Love*. At the studio, Jeff had to tickle Mitchell to get him giggling, that gurgling, gravelly kind of laugh that only babies can make. We captured it, added it to the recording, and now it's one of my favorite parts of the song. Daniel was singing his little three-year-old heart out along with me. I love hearing their little voices. They are growing up very quickly and I am appreciating this special time. Some day those two will become men who won't need their mommy anymore. I like that I am such an important part of their lives right now.
The home study is complete. There is now a full report about us in our adoption file. We passed the police and FBI checks and the agency has a good idea of who we are. We had to decide on whether we are open to a single referral or a sibling group, what age range, a boy or girl, etc. That was easy. But the medical portion of the questionnaire really got to me. What illnesses or conditions would we accept and what would we not accept? That was extremely difficult for me to answer, because I wanted to do the noble thing. In my mind, I was rationalizing, "Jeff is a physician. I'm a stay-

at-home mom. Maybe we should consider kids with more serious medical conditions. We can definitely afford it." I wrestled with myself for a long time about it, trying not to be selfish. I felt that God had been leading me so far, and I really wanted to do the right thing. It felt like every time I checked "NO" that I was turning away another child. I called a girlfriend, who had already adopted. "If you agree that you would accept a child with a severe condition, then that is probably what you are going to get. Special needs kids are the hardest to place. Be honest with yourself. What do *you* want?" Sarah told me the same thing. "Be brutally honest with yourself on this one. This is your family life and it is a forever commitment, so be completely clear about what *you* want, because it could be your reality."

I thought about what my life might be like if I had a child with significant medical problems. Would I be pushing one child in a wheelchair while chasing after Daniel and Mitch? Will there be many surgeries? Will these issues require most of my time? What will happen when this child becomes an adult and I'm still the caregiver? What will my daily life really be like? Would it be fair to the boys? The questions seemed unending.

Finally, I took a deep breath and wrote "healthy as possible" on the questionnaire. I still felt guilty about it, but in truth, a healthy baby was really what I wanted, and I had to decide what was best for me since I would be the one living with my choice. Also, I realized that there are no guarantees. God may give me a special needs child anyway. It's been said that God never gives us more than we can handle. I guess I'll just hope for the best situation.

The dossier paperwork that is required by the Russian government and the adoption agency is what we are working on now. There are so many documents, the stack is at least an inch and a half thick, and I am told that if there is even one mistake, there could be delays. No erasing, no whiteout allowed, and the forms must be completely typed except for signatures that must be notarized, then stamped and sealed by the state. The paperwork is unbelievable, but we must follow the Russian procedures exactly. I cannot help but wonder if our baby is even born yet, or if we will be together by next Christmas.

I want this process to move faster. I am working on the paperwork daily, but am barely halfway through it all. I'm waiting on everyone else to respond to our requests for things like employment verification, recent physicals, bank statements, a letter from our mortgage company, etc. It could take months to get this all together. Come on people, don't you realize how important this is? Let's get going!

My Ritual of Longing

April 1998

Hey, how about this news?

Daniel and Mitch and I had just gotten out of the pool at the hotel in Arizona. It had been a warm day at the medical convention. Our room phone was blinking . . . it was a message to call Sarah. I let the boys jump on the beds before I got them dressed. "Go ahead, you can jump, just be quiet, okay?" I asked. Jeff and I held the phone up between our ears. My heart started to pound as I heard Sarah's voice.

"We just got the call this morning. How do you feel about twins?" she said. I gasped and looked at Jeff. "Twins?" I gulped as I watched his jaw drop. We both stared at each other with our eyes open wide. "Yes, there were twin boys born on February 20th in Yaroslavl. They think they're identical. I can get a medical and a video to you within a week." As I fathomed the news, my blood pumped through the core of my stomach and into my head, like being on the first hill of a rollercoaster ride. Of course, we arranged to meet with her the second we get home. After we hung up, we just couldn't help ourselves . . . we were so excited that we joined our boys on the beds and jumped around together!

It's twins. Wow. How unbelievably amazing. I've always been thinking one. Now, there are two. I wish we could leave the conference early. I'm dying to see

them. Jeff is trying to stay calm, but he's excited too,
I can tell. Sarah will give us more information when
we get home. Then, we will make the decision. I'm
already thinking that this is it; I can't help it. It feels
like I just looked at a plus sign on a pregnancy test.
Breathe, Lori, breathe.

April 1998

Hi,

For so long, I've wondered about who my child is. Today,
it was confirmed for my heart. *These babies really do exist.*
We live on the same planet.

The video is less than two minutes long and is poor
quality. It begins with a freeze frame of what looks like two
Russian names and dates of birth, hand written on a piece
of paper. Then, it skips to a naked and crying baby lying on
several blankets. The baby is moving his little arms and legs
and crying heartily. The women in the room are speaking in
Russian so we don't understand what they are saying. I hold
my breath as I allow myself to become completely absorbed
in his pint-sized image on the TV screen. I am entranced
by this child immediately. I study his little bald head, tiny
hands, and feet. He has fair skin, like me. "Little Misha" is
what they have named him. The paperwork says that the film
was taken at one month of age, but he looks like a newborn
to me. There is barely any fat on his body. He's not round
like Dan and Mitch were at this age. I remind myself that he
was born early—six pounds at birth, which is pretty good for
thirty-six weeks of gestation.

As a woman begins to dress him, I notice that he has no
diaper, just a blanket wrapped in between and then around
his little legs. Sarah tells us that this cocoon wrapping is
common practice in European hospitals; they feel it helps the
babies to feel warm and secure, as in the womb. I notice that

his legs are very skinny. Suddenly, he tilts his tiny head to the side frantically. He is rooting, looking to nurse. He must be hungry. His crying dwindles as the woman dresses him in a white shirt that opens in the back. She quickly wraps more blankets around his legs, then wraps thicker blankets around the rest of him, and scoops him away.

Soon another woman wearing an apron and a tall white hat enters the room bringing in a smaller bundle of blankets. As she lays the bundle down, she unravels each layer until we see that there is a tiny, pink baby inside. "Etta Yaroslav," says the woman filming. I admire yet another beautiful bald head and tiny face on the screen. This one looks very preemie-like to me. There is no fat on him at all. It's clear that he has been asleep, and now that the woman is undressing him, he can barely muster a whimper. The paper says that this baby was four pounds at birth. She only takes off his little shirt, but leaves his legs wrapped in the blankets. "Why don't we see his legs?" says Jeff, with concern. The woman clicks her tongue and taps his tiny arm to get him to wake up. He then whimpers a little and turns his face towards the camera. His delicate features form into a smile. It melts me instantly. The tiny one's arms begin to shake until he cries hard. He must be getting cold. The woman hurriedly dresses him and bundles him back up into the tiny cocoon of blankets. Poof—the tape ends.

I feel cheated. I want more. I only got a few minutes to see each of them. It seemed like the women were in such a hurry. That's all there is of their introduction, a couple of names scratched on a piece of paper and less than two minutes of unclear footage, none of which has a close up. It seems so impersonal. Don't the women realize that we want to see as much as possible? I am exasperated. Still, I am intrigued beyond measure. I want more.

Both of them look no more than a week old to me, so I double check the paperwork. "One month old," it reads.

Neither of the babies has that cushy layer of fat that develops after a few weeks. I wonder if they are being fed or stimulated adequately. They are still beautiful to me. I hit rewind as Jeff and Sarah talk about the medical reports. There does not appear to be any serious ailments listed, but there are some typing errors that could go either way. As Jeff and Sarah discuss how we could have the reports checked out, I shush them both. I'm infatuated by the images. My eyes open wide as I watch again with complete concentration. I can feel my excitement building from deep within. *This is it.*

May 1998

Dear babies,

It has been so fun breaking the news to everyone in the family. Most of them have the same reaction: "What? Twins? Are you kidding? Wow! Awesome!"

My mom (your Nana) is very excited about this news and is already planning a twin baby shower. Now that we have accepted you as our referrals, we will need to wait until all the documents are approved by the Russian authorities. This could take many months, we are told. Your lives are now in their hands. It makes me uneasy to know that there could be delays. We have completed all that we can at our end and are just praying every day that we can get to you quickly. In the meantime, I watch your video every morning over coffee. Throughout the day, I share you with as many people who enter this house as possible. I wish I could somehow freeze frame the video into a photo or two that I could carry around. For some reason, the adoption agency never got your photographs with the medical report. So, I just keep a copy of the report in the side pocket of my purse. Only I know it's there. It sounds weird, but it's where I'm at right now. I need to feel closer to you. At night, your video is the last thing I watch before I go to bed. I've probably watched it at least a hundred times in the last two weeks. I've been closing my eyes and studying what your little voices sound like. It is becoming a secret obsession. We've decided to name you Craig Mikhail and Kevin Yaroslav. This way, your Russian names will be preserved. I think the names Craig and Kevin fit you perfectly.

May 1998

Hi babies,

I'm still waiting to hear word about when we can travel. You are now over two months old. I've painted your room in bright colors, yellow walls with plaid wallpaper and a children-of-the-world border. I want it as bright and busy as possible so it will stimulate you. I constantly wonder about you, what your day is like in the hospital, if you are being held regularly, and if there is enough for you to eat. There have been no new pictures or updates from the adoption agency. Sarah says "No news is good news." It's driving me nuts. I want to get there to you *now*. Every day that goes by is another day that you don't have the best care possible — me.

Daniel and Mitchell know all about you. We talk about you every day, and the boys know that you did not grow in my tummy like they did and that we will have to take a long trip to get you. They seem to be really excited about being big brothers. I sense that they will be open to you. Now, every time they see a plane in the sky, they say, "Look, Mommy, somebody's going to Russia."

June 1998

Hello my babies. I've resorted to carrying this letter with me daily, so I can look at it and think of you.

Dear Kevin and Craig,

Your room has fresh paint, and it's almost ready for you. I steal away every chance I get to close the door for a little quiet time to think and plan. Then, I dust the rocking chair and fiddle with your crib blankets before I finally sit. It's what I call my ritual of longing.

Here is my place to be alone in the lull and dream of you. I close my eyes, and imagine that my mind can drift across the ocean to be with you. I wonder what you're feeling at this very moment, across the world. Are you sleeping? Are you crying? Are your arms stretched out? Are you waiting too?

Waiting is what they tell us we have to do. It doesn't seem fair that you're there and I'm here when we need each other so much. I find myself crying all the time, just missing you. I try not to show it, because I haven't even met you, but I yearn to be with you. I ache inside. All I can do is pray that God will keep you safe.

Here in this room with fresh paint, I think of her, the young woman who gave you life. She is your birth mother. She endured pain and tremendous sacrifice in choosing to let you live. Her heartbreak in letting you go has allowed you to be free. Boys, you must always respect her for this ultimate gift. Even though the two of us are strangers, I still feel an unusual sort of bond with her just in knowing that we have both shed tears over you. Maybe she's also found a place to go off and dream of you both.

I'm so excited for you to meet your brothers and your daddy. Our whole family celebrates in even the promise of you. They can't wait to surround you with love. What a beautiful blessing it will be for me to share them all with you. You will grow up knowing that *you were wanted.*

There is so much uncertainty in life; for me, making decisions has been a little scary at times. However, my faith consoles me. After all, God has led me on this path to you

and He will lead you to me. Our souls were meant to meet—
it's part of His plan for us. God will give me what He knows
I can manage and so I know whatever comes, we'll handle
it—together. The important thing is that like your older
brothers, your lives will be full and you will be loved—and
it is my life's work to make that happen for you.

Someday if you have questions, I will help you understand
how you came to be. I promise to tell you everything I know
about your birth family and to not hold anything back. Never
doubt your special place in this family. You will always be,
in the deepest sense, my sons . . . each unique and beautiful in
your own way.

So when you're finally here in this room with fresh
paint, we'll share a little quiet time together. I look forward
to singing you to sleep in the rocking chair and looking
down into your sweet faces. At last, you'll be home with us,
my ritual of longing will be over, and your new lives will
begin.

I love you,
Mom

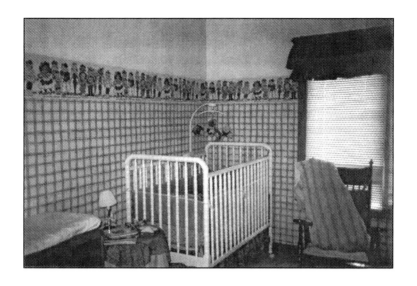

The freshly-painted room.

Into the Unknown

⌒

July 10, 1998

12:50 AM (USA)
8:50 AM (Russia)

Good morning, babies,

The trip from Detroit to New York was only a couple of hours. We're now on the ten-hour flight to Moscow. Then, tomorrow we will take a train (four hours) to the city of Yaroslavl, where you are. I can't believe we're finally on our way. Saying goodbye to Daniel and Mitch was more difficult than I expected. I managed to hide my emotions while I was with them, but I cried as we pulled away. This is the first time I will be apart from them for so long. It took a few minutes for that pain in the core of my stomach to go away. But I also know that we are on a positive mission. This is a huge adventure and I intend to soak up as much of the experience as I can. I am on a quest to meet you, my babies.

The adoption agency arranged for us to travel with another couple adopting from the same region. We met Kris and John at JFK Airport. They will be adopting a baby girl and are just as excited as us. It's been nice to be able to share our thoughts with them. Kris and I talked for an hour on this flight about how we got to this place in our lives. While I listened to her, I noticed her eyes opening very wide while she spoke. I could tell that she was completely immersed emotionally in the anticipation and excitement of meeting her daughter for the first time. She too had a biological son, so we shared openly about our maternal connection with our children and how close that bond really is. She too has been allowing her heart to open to this new child whom she has never met. She confided to me that she carried around a picture of her in her pocket for months, just to feel close. *I guess I'm not so weird after all.*

After a time, my mind began to wander over to you once again. I acknowledged Kris as I watched her lips move, but I allowed my thoughts to travel to that surreal place, playing over and over again the scene of when I first hold you. As I pretended to listen, I pondered about not wearing any perfume on the day we meet, so that you can get to know my natural scent immediately. I want to know your smell and have it be second nature to me, much like Dan and Mitch. It's that motherly primal-instinctive thing. I'm so ready to find out everything I can about all your little quirks. . . things that only moms recognize in their babies. I can't help but constantly think of you. *In two days, I'll be touching you.*

July 11, 1998

Dear me,
This is another world . . . Russia is different. I immediately felt uncomfortable when we left the plane and there was nothing written in English. Jeff and I huddled close together as we followed the crowds to the baggage claim. I noticed immediately that people barely speak to one another, but just push their way through the line. I felt that if I needed help from anyone, I wouldn't get it. It's every man for himself. Now I have a bit of an understanding of how foreign people must feel when they come to the United States—very alone and very vulnerable in a foreign land.

I have been watching the people here intently. I sense a kind of cast over them, and it's grey in color. Not too many in this society smile, even outside the airport. Young women walk on the street with their arms locked together, which is not common back home. Still, they don't talk or laugh together. People look to me as if they are late for work and have a lot on their minds. I saw a man pull out a crust of bread from his pocket and eat it. It wasn't a sandwich, or a snack wrapped in plastic like we have back home, but a plain piece of bread with a hard crust. That was it. Like many of the men here, he had a very strong body odor.

The clothing is different here too. I haven't noticed bright colors on anyone except young women, who have a very sexy look. Most are very thin, with silky tank tops, tight jeans, and high heels. No one wears shorts, even though it's ninety degrees. A heavyset older woman with an olive green suit and pointy-toed ankle boots gave me a dirty look as I stood next to her. I'm wearing loose jeans and tennis shoes and definitely don't look like the other women around here. We stick out, and it has given me an uneasy feeling.

Finally, we got to the train station, where we met Lilia, who works for the adoption agency. We will be staying with her family in their apartment, and she will accompany us to the hospital tomorrow. She looks to be my age, and is very naturally beautiful and athletic looking, with short blonde hair and brown eyes. *I wonder what kind of life she lives.* I am interested in seeing her apartment and meeting her husband and young son, who is Daniel's age.

About an hour out of Moscow, I observed the country-side as we sped past. Most of what I saw were clusters of small shack-like homes with dirt roads between them. I noted metal roofs on the houses, with shutters on the windows painted the same blue color. Some of the little houses had gardens, and there were old fences around most of the home-steads. There were no stores, gas stations, or paved roads on this route. Cows walked openly on the dirt roads. I couldn't believe the difference in this environment, compared to the hustle and bustle of Moscow. It looked like we've stepped back in time at least forty years. To see Russia from this perspective made me even more curious about how things will look at Lilia's apartment.

The Russian countryside.

Lilia seemed very pleasant but quiet. She could speak only a few words in English, but she did manage to give us an update that Misha and Yaroslav are both healthy, strong, and smiling babies. We couldn't do much communicating on the train, so we spent a great deal of time awkwardly smiling at each other and looking out the window in silence. I wondered what she thinks of us. She knows we are here on a good will mission to pick up our babies. It's all good. We don't need to explain. I am feeling strong in my conviction to become a mother again.

I knew it was going to happen eventually. I needed to pee. Finding the restroom wasn't difficult at all. It was located in the center of the train. Thankfully, there wasn't a long line. I made sure to steady myself over the bowl and not accidentally sit, as the ride was very wobbly. When I finished, I pulled the chord above. Then, WHOOSH! The basin opened to a blast of air, and I could see the tracks below, moving at top speed. *Oh geez, I just christened the tracks!* I wondered how many hundreds of others had also. *Gross!*

Finally, we pulled into Yaroslavl, which was a bustling city not as big as Moscow, but a city just as well with apartment buildings, businesses, and restaurants. The main roads had wires hanging above them. Streetcar-looking busses connected to those wires as they traveled along. Every large tree along the roads was painted white at the base. It didn't appear that anyone cuts grass regularly. The ground was mostly weeds and cracked cement. Stray dogs were everywhere. Even the road signs looked unusual; no English. People walked about with angry looks on their faces, and once again, they did not look at each other or speak. Everyone seemed to be in a hurry to get wherever they were going. The few young children I saw held hands with their adults in an orderly manner. The heat reflecting off the street seemed sweltering, but most everyone was wearing long pants. The younger women dressed sexy, like in Moscow, either short skirts or tight jeans and very high spiky heels. Most everyone was of slim build. The only heavier people were the older women in babushkas, wearing dingy dresses or old skirts and scuffed shoes with men's socks. The old people sat on benches on the corners of the street to sell sunflower seeds and cigarettes. I took it all in. *I feel like such a foreigner, at the mercy of Lilia and the people here. We definitely will just be gracious and do what we are told.*

When we got to Lilia's apartment, we noticed her building was dirty and falling apart. A building like this would only be found in the projects back in the U. S. I could smell urine and mold as we made our way up the filthy stairway to her second-floor apartment. Surprisingly, I was delighted at how well kept and clean it was on the inside. There was a small entranceway with five doorways, each opening to a separate little room. The kitchen was the first room on the right. On the wall above the dinette table hung the word "Welcome" in English. *Good, other American families have been here so we are not the first.* Lilia led us to the next room that was their main living area. It was decorated with deep green floral wallpaper. An oriental rug hung from the main wall. The room contained a sofa bed, two makeshift cribs, a small side table, and a chair. A set of double windows provided a warm breeze and a view of the street below.

Soon, her husband Kolya entered the room and kindly shook our hands. "Nyet En-glay-skee," he said. No English. "Nyet Roos-kee-ah," added Jeff. No Russian. Both men smiled at each other. Lilia introduced their son Dima, who peeped out from behind his father's legs, smiling shyly. It startled me that his teeth were rotted and turning black, so I tried not to stare. This is another thing I've noticed about many Russian people; they don't have decent dental work. The man with the bread at the airport in Moscow had only two gold front teeth. The rest were missing.

As a family, they showed us to door number three which was the bathroom. The fourth door led into a small bedroom which they shared when visitors came. The last room was a small den with bookshelves and a couple of chairs and lamps. This was their home. We will be comfortable here for the next four days. This is awesome, to be living with a real Russian family, experiencing their home life firsthand, eating their food, trying to communicate, observing their lifestyle. I'm intrigued by these people and I will let their culture soak in. *I wonder what they think of us.*

Meeting You

July 12

My sweet babies,

    I barely slept last night in anticipation of today, the day that I have been dreaming about. Dad and I tossed and turned most of the night, and ended up sitting up in bed talking until 4 AM. We just couldn't sleep. Of course, it didn't help that there was barely a breeze coming through the window. Our room was so hot and stuffy it was almost unbearable. As morning broke, we ate a small breakfast of potato cakes, cottage cheese, and raisins. Then our driver took us to Hospital #3: your home for the last four-and-a-half months.

    As the car pulled up, I noticed that there was no parking lot or walkway to the entrance of the children's section. Weeds grew where there should have been grass. The building itself was old, and obviously poor. The upper windows were open and did not have screens. The tall wooden entrance door was heavy and squeaked as we opened it. As we entered, I noticed a metal bucket full of foamy cow's milk next to the doorway. Our translator explained that neighboring farms donate the milk to help feed the babies. I wondered how long it had been sitting there uncovered in the heat.

Hospital #3, with its wooden door.

We were led to a small room. Lilia grabbed the video camera and began filming the two of us standing there smiling as we waited for the nurse to bring you in. It seemed like I could hear my own heart beating; I could feel it pounding in my chest.

Suddenly, the door opened and a doctor came in, holding a beautiful bald baby with wide blue eyes. You, Kevin, were clinging to the doctor as she passed you to me. You looked around, bobbing your head up and down, trying to hold it up to take in your surroundings. Once your eyes focused on me, you smiled happily. As soon as I was able to grab on to you, I kissed you on the cheek. Amazingly, my vocabulary went dead in the excitement of the moment. All I could say was "Hi. I'm your mommy. Hi."

I stood there holding you, swaying you back and forth, and looked into your big wide eyes. You smiled at me again. Dad and I surrounded you with our arms as we passed you back and forth, cooing with you. To be touching your soft skin and feeling your sweet breath on my face ignited all of my senses. I took you in like oxygen. Dad and I admired you and just giggled to each other; because neither of us could muster any kind of intelligent comment. It was just total awe.

Soon, the doctor entered the room again, this time carrying another bald-headed baby who bobbed his head and looked around in the same way as the first. "Etta Misha," the doctor said. You, Craig, clung to the doctor as she passed you over to Dad. Those big eyes of yours took him in and you latched onto his shirt with your tiny hands. *It amazes me how trusting little babies are . . . it's a beautiful thing to see.* We held you up next to each other with your heads together and laughed. Our translator said: "Same face." You both looked exactly alike! I just had to kiss your cheek in the same spot that I had kissed Kevin. I slowly breathed you in. Once again, all I could say was a soft, "Hi. I'm Mommy." You, Craig, were a little bit bigger than Kevin, and when you looked at me, our eyes locked. The skin on my arms began to goose bump, and I could feel an exhilarating quiver travel up my spine. I was really and truly touching you! I became completely engrossed in the moment. It was like a dream—we were finally together.

Lori, Craig, Kevin, and Jeff; together at last!

Dad and I awkwardly practiced passing you both back and forth at the same time, constantly switching babies. Next, we laid you both next to each other on the table and began to undress you. Our translator pointed out that you both had cradle cap, a crusty irritation on your scalp. As I played with you, Dad did a very discreet version of the doctor's health check. The first thing he did was uncover legs. For months, we had wondered about those legs on Kevin, because the video never showed them. As I continued to tickle your tummies, he whispered, "Looks like they are okay." The two of us smiled and gave each other a gentle kiss. It reminded me of the same kind of kiss we shared at the births of Daniel and Mitchell, one of life's special moments.

As we examined you next to each other, we were stunned as to how exactly alike you actually looked. We agreed that we needed to have some sort of plan as to how to tell you apart. I was pleased that now you seemed much healthier than the way you looked on the video. You both had at least an inch of fat on you. You were also much more alert than I expected. You looked around the room like it was a very new place. I wondered how long you were in your previous room, and if you had ever made it out, until now. You both gurgled with delight when I touched you and stroked your cheeks. I just couldn't keep my hands off you. I constantly kissed each of you on my favorite place on babies; that soft space right under the ear. I whispered, "I'm your mommy" to you both as we played with you and touched you.

With Lilia looking on, Lori tells Craig, "I'm your mommy."

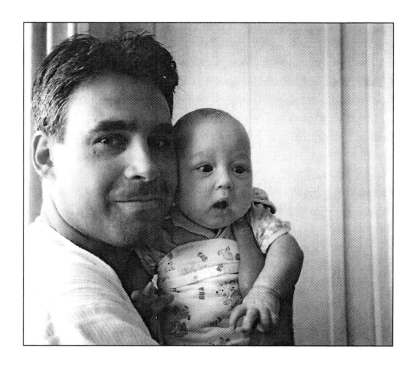

Jeff holds Kevin proudly.

Time seemed to fly by while we loved you up and took pictures together. All too soon, our translator said that it was time to go. We had been with you for forty-five minutes. That's all that was allowed for the first meeting. I felt cheated, but we complied and gave you back to the doctor. As I watched the doctor carry you off, it occurred to me that you would probably be going back to that same room you had always been in. I whispered to myself under my breath, "Not for long." Tomorrow we will visit you again after court, and take you out of the hospital and into your new lives.

July 13

Dear sons,

   We got an early start this rainy morning. When we arrived at the hospital, Dad gave the administrator some gifts: needles, syringes, and antibiotics. She was extremely grateful. We then took you into town to get your passport pictures taken. They had dressed you in heavy cotton pajamas and little white hats that looked like bonnets. It was eighty-five degrees! I knew that you would sweat, but we didn't say anything. In the car, I unsnapped the front of your outfits and studied your faces, trying to find something different about each of you. It was really hard to tell you apart. Our plan was to always hold the same baby when traveling, so Dad and I kept re-assuring each other about which one we were holding. "You have Kevin, I have Craig," I said. I was afraid that we would get you mixed up and you would forever have the wrong identity! At the passport office, I pinned a safety pin onto Craig's pajamas, because the photographer was also having difficulty telling you apart. The camera he used was so old, it actually went "poof" when he snapped the picture, and a puff of smoke came out of it! We waited for about an hour, and then got your photos. Sure enough, they looked like antique pictures.

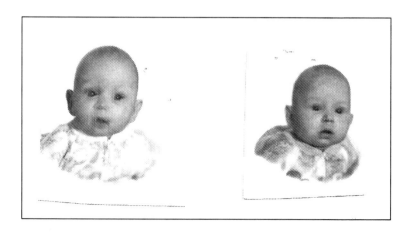

Passport photos.

We drove you back to the hospital, dropped you off, and headed for the courthouse. I was very nervous about the court appearance and desperately afraid that the judge would not grant us the adoption for whatever reason. Even though all of the paperwork was in order, and we passed all the background checks, the decision was ultimately hers. That the rest of your lives were in her hands gave me a sinking feeling.

The courtroom I had imagined was really nothing more than an office. The judge entered the room looking stern. She was a young woman of thirty-two. My mouth went dry as she asked us to stand. She asked each of us a few questions through our translator. "What kind of education will you provide for these children? Do you both work outside the home? Will you treat them differently from your other children?" As I gave her my answers, I just couldn't hold back my emotions. I choked back tears as I promised to be the best mother I could be to you. I wished I hadn't been so emotional, but I just couldn't help it. After all the months of waiting, we had made it all the way to this moment, and the intensity of it all just came spilling out of me. Thankfully, she understood. It must not have been the first time she watched adoptive parents sobbing in her courtroom. She approved the adoption, we signed some papers, and that was it. The whole thing took about fifteen minutes.

The rest of the afternoon, we drove around from building to building all over the city, waiting in lines in stuffy rooms for more official signatures and special seals. We obtained the adoption certificates, new birth certificates with our names listed as the parents, and Russian passports. Finally, it was time to carry you out of the hospital.

I brought special outfits for you for this important day. Little blue striped onesies with matching caps. We took some more pictures together. They would not allow us to enter or take photographs of the room that you had lived in for the last four-and-a-half months. The doctor came in, thanking us once again for the medicines. I took that opportunity to ask her some questions about your birth mother: 1.65 meters in height, normal weight, blonde hair, blue eyes; a seamstress, unmarried, has a child the age of three, a girl. She signed off parental rights immediately. There was no information about the birth father, except that he was a bricklayer with brown hair, of average height and weight. I asked if the twins had ever been in the same crib together. "No." Did the babies ever go outside? "No, they have never seen the sun." We covered your little legs cocoon-style to keep up with the Russian tradition. Dad held Kevin and I held Craig as usual as we said our thank yous and goodbyes, and boldly walked out that squeaky wooden door.

Leaving the hospital: Lori, Craig, Kevin, Jeff.

A sense of calm and peace took over my body as I breathed in the fresh air outside. The rainy morning had turned into a beaming, summer afternoon, so we covered your heads with a blanket to protect your eyes from the extreme brightness. "You're going into the light honey," I whispered into your blanket as I walked to the car. What an amazing feeling to be finally leaving Hospital #3 with you in my arms. For a second, I lifted my head to feel the warmth of the sun on my face, and I imagined that it was God touching me. I knew He was there, with His hand wrapped around us in safety. Everything was going to be all right. I could feel the soft embrace of His peace.

Lilia was happy to see us as we arrived at the apartment. She had prepared dinner for us, but first, it was time for you to have a bath, a bottle, and a nap. I couldn't wait to just dig into being your mom and taking care of all your needs. Dad asked Lilia for some red nail polish, and I immediately painted Craig's big toenail. Now we would be able to tell you apart more easily and there will be no identity mix-ups! We laid you next to each other in one of the makeshift cribs. You both sucked your right thumbs and fell asleep within moments of each other in exactly the same position. Once you were tucked away, we sat at the dinner table and shared our day with Lilia.

Finally, now that this day is over and you are asleep and content, I am able to write this. What an important day this has been. *You are officially ours. I feel incredibly strong. Goodnight my babies.*

Reality Strikes

July 14

Hi, my boys,

We all woke up this morning with itchy red spots all over us. Mine were on my legs. Your spots were all over your faces and upper bodies. At first, I assumed that they were mosquito bites, but after Dad took a look, we realized what they were. Bedbugs! The furniture is so old in Lilia's apartment; it's no wonder that there are creepy crawlies inside the cushions. Unfortunately, there is no place else for you to sleep except in the crib. We recovered your crib mattresses with extra towels, and covered your spots with anti-itch lotion. I didn't complain about it to Lilia. She looked exhausted. *Just a few more days to go and we'll be out of here.*

Today was my day to practice taking care of two babies at a time, alone. Now was the time to test myself to make sure I can successfully manage, so by the time we get home, I can add Dan and Mitch to the mix. I've learned how to deal with one four month old, but two at once? This would take some practice. I sent Dad out shopping with the driver. He was glad to get out of the small stuffy apartment for a little while. I laid out your clothes and set up your bottles before you woke up. The pre-planning worked. To my surprise, I was able to get you bathed, dressed, and fed inside of forty-

five minutes—*not bad for one person with no help. I did it!
I can handle this. It feels good.*

I've already noticed many things about you. You are both
thumb suckers and you can hold your own bottle and roll
over. Your legs are a little weak and you are much smaller
than Daniel and Mitchell were at four months. Coming from
an institution, it is expected that you will have delays. You
both respond to my voice and my touch. You smile and coo
at me. I can tell that although you probably had less stimula-
tion than most babies, you were held from time to time in
those months. I am grateful that you are very alert and happy
babies.

After playtime, I laid you next to each other on your backs
in one crib. As I organized your clothes, you got very quiet,
so I stood still and watched your crib from across the room.
Then an amazing thing happened. In perfect union, both sets
of your little hands rose into the air. As you lay there silently,
your wrists flipped palms up, then palms down, simultane-
ously. The movement reminded me of synchronized swim-
mers, so precisely equal. It occurred to me that this was how
you must have entertained yourselves when you were alone
in your cribs for all those months in the hospital; just looking
at the front and back of your hands. I carefully crept up to
your crib and peeped over the top. You both saw me and
smiled at exactly the same time. I lifted my head over your
faces and took both of Craig's hands into my right hand, and
Kevin's hands into my left. As I gurgled baby talk to you, I
could feel my tears welling up in my eyes. "You will never
have to play with your hands again. I'm here. I love you, my
babies," I said as my tears dropped onto your faces, dotting
your cheeks. You both blinked as the drops came down, as
if you were in a rain shower. At that instant, I realized that
as your mother, I was finally able to meet one of your primal
needs, the need to be touched. Instead of you reaching your
hands up to find nothing, you reached up and found me. It

was the precious moment that I had been yearning for. In that little room within the privacy of just the three of us, I allowed my emotions to let go and pour out without hesitation. My rain shower of tears came down onto you. I felt safe in letting my heart open to you even more than before. In that moment, I felt the bond between us becoming stronger and deeper. My connection with you was being formed.

I can feel my maternal pull to you. It's much like how I had felt with Daniel and Mitch. However, this is different. With them, for months, I had felt their every kick and movement inside me, a familiar presence in my body and soul. As soon as they were born, our bond was instant because of that intimacy. As I am experiencing you, I am feeling that same bond happening more slowly, and I am relishing every moment of it. I can actually feel our inner selves opening to each other. *I'm not afraid . . . I'm letting you in.*

This afternoon, Lilia wanted to feed you both some mashed potatoes mixed with whole milk. I didn't think your digestive systems were quite ready, but I accepted her generosity and didn't argue. You both ate a tiny bit from a spoon, and Lilia was happy. She enjoyed feeding you. It's a woman thing, to nurture the children that come into your home. I get that, and I smiled as I watched her with the two of you.

I like Lilia. She is intelligent, she's naturally beautiful, and she is strong. Her life is much more difficult than mine. I've learned a lot about her just by observing. I have noticed that her husband does not help with any household chores or cooking. She makes the eight-hour roundtrip train ride and then opens her home for adoptive families. She takes care of their son and maintains the entire apartment. Her work never seems to end. Last night, she was up at 1:00 AM. on her hands and knees scrubbing the floors. The translator told me that she was the one filming your first video that I have watched hundreds of times. Now, I have a better perspective of who she is and all she has done to help us. She and I can't speak to each other very well, but we understand each other just the same. I appreciate her kindness and her work ethic. We respect our individual differences, and although she lives a life that is not similar to mine, I know that we want the same things for our families. *We are all human, no matter where we come from.*

We've got one more day here in Yaroslavl, and I intend to soak up as much of this place as I can. I am learning all I can about you both and I feel fortunate that I have had some time to be alone with you and really get to know you. I want to know everything about you.

July 16

Dear Kevin and Craig,

After exchanging gifts, we said goodbye to Lilia and her family today. She and I shared a tearful, long hug at the train station. She has done so much to help us. I am grateful for her generosity. We waved your hands goodbye as we stepped onto the train.

I watched the countryside as we sped along. There were many clusters of shacks and tiny homes that made up small villages. Occasionally, I'd see a person walking down a dirt road, bent over a small garden, or standing next to a pile of watermelons, as if to be guarding it. Not many people smile here. I haven't seen anyone laugh in a week. The general mood is sullen. *People look like they are quietly suffering.*

Dad and I took turns letting each of you look out the window on the four-hour train ride back to Moscow. As we traveled further and further away from your first home, I couldn't help but wonder if and when we'd be back. Maybe someday when you are older, we can all visit together as a family. I wondered about your biological sister, and what she was doing at that very moment. I wondered about your mother, if she was thinking about you or sensing that you were drifting farther away. Silently, I prayed for them.

Jeff and Kevin look out the window.

Once in Moscow, our driver took us to a huge apartment complex that looked like it was crumbling, our next home-stay. There we met Ira, a large woman in her late forties with a booming voice and a huge heart. She immediately started fussing over you both as soon as we hit the door. When she hugged me, she squeezed me so tightly, it took my breath away.

Her apartment was very clean and tidy, with more modern amenities. *We'll get to watch TV here, which is a nice change.* Ira works as a nanny and has a grown son, so she lives alone. She spoke only a few words of English. "… Lordia (Lori), no problem, okay, no sleep, eat, good…" I couldn't help but like her and let her take charge of us all.

Our dinner was chicken gizzards with cabbage. I didn't want to offend her, but I thought I might gag, so I shot Jeff a "please help me" look and as soon as she left the room, he ate my portion. Luckily, she stored a bucket of homemade dill pickles on her back porch, so I filled up on them.

The rest of the day and night, we settled into our new place and played with you both. You are advancing very quickly—rolling over with ease. I decided to lay you both onto your tummies facing each other. You lifted your heads and looked at each other with wonder and surprise. I was able to snap the moment on film. It looked like you were looking at each other for the first time!

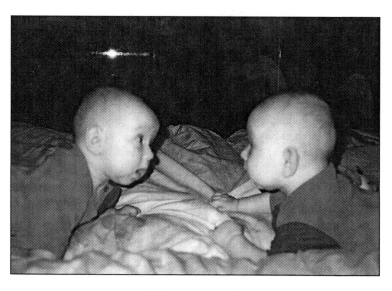

"Who are you?"

Since day one of being your mom, I have kept you together in the same crib. With everything I've read about the bond of twins, I feel that you need to be near enough to touch each other. I can't believe that the hospital put you into separate cribs for four-and-a-half months. You had never even been introduced to each other until the day we met you! The two of you noticing each other today was a first, and I was there to experience it. I am feeling fortunate once again.

July 18

Guess what;

Today we learned that our traveling companions Kris and John are heading home early. Apparently, they were pretty insistent with the adoption agency that they need to get home *now* because their son is sick with strep throat. Having bent some rules, they went to the embassy and got their daughter's visa yesterday. This was a huge inconvenience for the translator who had to stay up until 2:00AM. to finish typing their documents. We were told that they did not even say thank you when they left abruptly.

I hope that this doesn't damage U. S. /Russian relations for other adoptions. Overall, Russians think that Americans are pushy and demanding. I can understand how they would feel that way. In America, we live in a microwave society where we expect to expedite our business quickly. In Russia, people wait in line all day to get one document signed. It's their way of life. "We will wait," is the mindset.

Kevin was really constipated today, probably because of the potatoes Lilia gave him a few days ago. He was crying and crying. Ira got on the phone in a flash, trying to obtain just the right medicine to help. She ran out the door and quickly came back with some sort of herbal remedy in a bottle. At first, I was a little skeptical because we could not read the label and we had *no* idea what the stuff was. Was it for infants? What if he was allergic to it? After about ten minutes of her trying to explain the ingredients to me with Kevin screaming on my lap, I just decided to trust her and give him the medicine.

Together, Ira and I took off his diaper and laid him on the bed, holding his little legs in the air. It was quite the picture, both of us at each side of him talking over his face in our own languages: "C'mon, you can do it," and "Poshlee, cocket, Kevin" (meaning, "Let's go poop, Kevin"). We both shrieked excitedly and held our breath in unison as his tiny face turned red and he began to push. Suddenly, a small nugget the size of an almond popped out. The two of us squealed in delight and hugged each other over his little body. Soon, he released the rest of it, so fast that it splattered all over the bedspread.

Ira didn't mind. She nodded her head proudly, saying "Da, cocket, Kevin" (meaning, "Yes, Kevin pooped"). I thanked her profusely. I'm glad I trusted her. She is a very loving woman, and so fun to be with. Any time one of the babies makes a peep, she rushes into the room to scoop him up. Jeff has gotten caught in his underwear a few times already, but it doesn't seem to faze her at all. She's like a mom to us too, cooking for us and making sure we have everything we need. Yesterday, she noticed a zit on my nose that I thought no one could see. She pointed to her nose and said, "Lordia . . . problem?" and passed me her special pimple cream. *Nothing gets past this woman...*

It felt so good to talk to Daniel and Mitchell today. As soon as I heard Dan say, "Hi, Mommy," I teared up. I've never been away from them for so long. I miss them. We put the babies' ears to the phone so they could talk. It will be an awesome reunion when we finally get home. Everyone will come to the airport to greet us, and then we'll have a house full of people to celebrate with.

It's hard to believe that we are now a family of six. I'm glad that I've had the time to really get in tune with both babies alone first without having to divide my time with the boys. I wonder how it will be when we settle in at home. I'll have four boys under the age of five, every day. Jeff will be at work or outside doing things, so I'll be the main caregiver. I'll be singing on the weekends with the band. I know I can make it work. I feel very strong in my conviction that I will handle it.

This evening, we got a call from the agency rep. There is a delay with our embassy paperwork and we will now need to stay in Moscow for two additional days. It's out of our hands, so we will wait. *It doesn't seem fair that Kris and John broke the rules and left early, and we have to stay even longer.* Oh well, after our time here, I've learned to just go with the flow. Looking at the bright side, at least we will be able to do some sightseeing and soak up more of the culture. And I can have more of Ira's pickles. I've become addicted to them.

We've bought lots of Russian things for our house so that Kevin and Craig will have a sense of their heritage. I've read that it is very important to keep the culture alive and acknowledge it regularly. After all, Russia is where they come from. Their home, however, will be with us.

July 20

Hello my babies,

You are five months old today! We've been gone ten days and are finally on our last night in Russia. *I want to go home.*

It was extremely hot and humid today. I slathered on lots of sunscreen and dressed you in lightweight cotton onesies with ball caps. You liked feeling the breeze and open air on you. As we carried you in our arms on our way to the embassy, I was stopped several times by Russian women, disapprovingly telling me to cover your legs and wrap you in blankets. Apparently, it is unacceptable to even bring babies outside, let alone show any skin, even in ninety-degree weather! It only reminded me of how differently we think. I was glad to get you outside, especially after being in that hospital for four-and-a-half months, breathing that same stale air.

All went well at the embassy. Unlike the horror stories we had heard before we came here, obtaining your visas only took about two hours. You are now cleared to enter the United States. *Whew!* It was the last official process we had to go through in getting you home.

Tonight, we shared one more meal with Ira. We thanked her for her kindness, and gave her some gifts, including some money. She didn't want to take it, but we insisted. We know that she struggles, like everyone else here. It was the least we could do. Tearfully, she accepted, and the five of us group-hugged. She then carried each of you off separately to talk to you and say a private goodbye. *Once again, I am admiring a woman who is so different, yet so similar. God bless you, Ira. I will never forget you.*

Heading Home

July 21

My babies,

We're eight-and-a-half hours into the flight to New York. Dad and I walked you up and down the aisle until your eyelids got sluggish and you drifted off to dreamland. Finally, you are snoozing comfortably on your blankets right next to me as I write this. This will probably be the last time I can sit down and write out my thoughts. It'll be a whirlwind of activity when we get home. Daniel and Mitch will be waiting for us at the airport, along with Nana and Papa, Grandma and Grandpa, your aunts, uncles, cousins, and our closest friends. I can't wait for everyone to meet you.

There are many adopted kids on this flight. Talking with various other parents on this same journey has been a special pleasure for me. *They get it.* I met a really nice couple who adopted a delicate little girl from Siberia. I guessed her to be around eighteen months, but was shocked to find out that she was actually three years old. She was frail, due to malnutrition, and seemed restless and very distant emotionally. She did not want to engage much with anyone and rocked back and forth on the seat. I've read that many institutionalized children rock to comfort themselves when there is no one there to hold. Thank God that little girl has been saved, but she has a long way to go to catch up. Her parents looked relieved to finally have her, but also worried about what lies ahead. I said a silent prayer for their family.

I am grateful that you both are so responsive, and that you are healthier than we expected. "Healthy as possible" is what we hoped for, and thankfully, God gave us two thriving sons. Each day you are getting stronger. You are progressing at amazing speed. *We are blessed.*

You are both such sweet and delicious babies. I like to snuggle my face into your tiny necks to make you giggle and squeal with delight. Because Dad and I have been moving your legs every day, they have become stronger, more flexible, and not as stiff as they were before. I'm finding myself pretend-chewing on your feet and the outside of your thighs, a habit that formed when Daniel and Mitchell were this age. You both respond to my voice and you look into my eyes when I speak to you. That is one thing that I appreciate about you and all babies . . . your ability to look into a person's soul through their eyes. You have nothing to hide, no shame, and no fear. You are just totally open beings. You've already looked into me, and I took you in. We are now connected. There is no more distance between us. You are mine and I am yours.

As I'm admiring you as you sleep, I am treasuring what an amazing adventure this has been. The people that we have encountered left a lasting impression on us. Strangers that grew to be friends. They worked so hard to help us, giving you the chance at a better life.

I can't help but reminisce about those early months of anticipation, when I would sit in your freshly painted room and secretly allow the tears to flow. Waiting for you to come into my life seemed like an eternity. For a long time, I felt a hole from deep within my most personal self. The intense longing that I carried around before I met you was very real. At times, I felt an undeniable pain deep in my gut, which surprised me. Physically, my body was responding in a way that defied my own common sense. I questioned myself constantly, wondering why I was yearning so desperately for someone I didn't even know. I told no one about it, because I assumed that others couldn't possibly understand it. Now, I want to share this incredible experience with everyone.

Completely accepting you as my children didn't happen in a flash like a lightning strike, but over an extended period of many months. I believe that God planned the timing of this process just for me. Perhaps I needed to work through my own fears of the unknown, and He knew what it would take.

I now realize that my soul was beginning to love you and let you in before we had ever met. My heart knew it before my head knew it. My human brain needed time to truly understand so that I could take the leap of faith that God had planned for me all along.

Any anxiety and worry that I carried for all that time has now been replaced by an overwhelming sense of joy and relief. It feels so good to cry because I'm so happy. God gave me a wonderful sense of peace that I can feel deep down. It's my own personal witness, and a gift from Him.

I used to think coming full circle as a woman meant I needed to give birth. Now I realize that being a complete woman is about loving the way God intended me to love. I am so lucky to have experienced all of it. The void has been filled. Now that we are finally together, and our hearts have opened to each other, the circle of our family grows bigger and bigger. I am forever blessed because He picked us for each other. I love you. Here we go, my loves. We're almost home.

Stepping off the plane and into a new life...

Brothers at last! Mitchell holds Craig; Daniel holds Kevin.

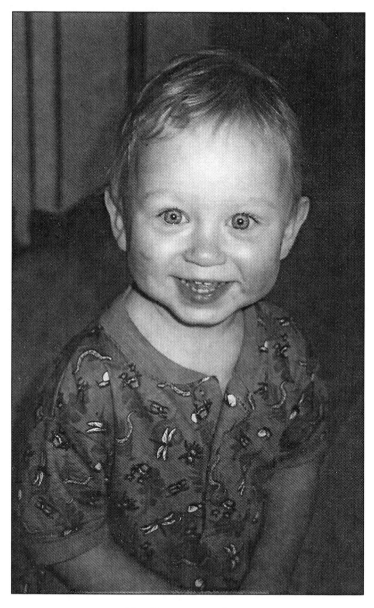

Kevin one year later

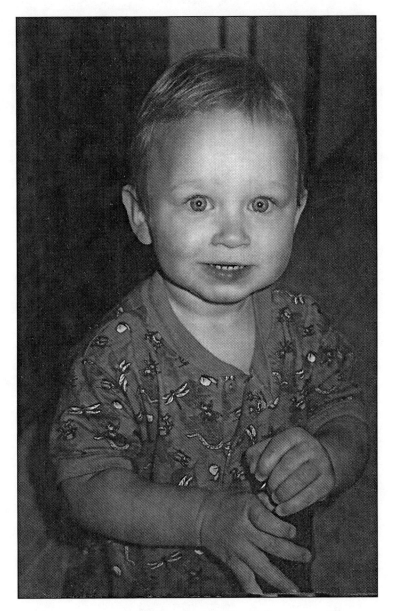

Craig one year later

Craig and Kevin at three years old.

For family updates, visit http://www.loriadams.net.

Printed in the United States
88582LV00003B/1-468/A

9 781602 667549